A HIDDEN GARDEN

A Hidden Garden

*The Poems of
Whitley Strieber*

A Hidden Garden is a Walker & Collier book,
Copyright © 2024, Walker & Collier, Inc.
Walker & Collier Inc 20742 Stone Oak Parkway Suite 107,
San Antonio, Texas, 78258
First Walker & Collier printing, first edition, 2024

All rights reserved. This book or parts thereof may not be reproduced in any form without permission. Library of Congress Cataloging-in-Publication Data Strieber, Whitley

A Hidden Garden / by Whitley Strieber ISBNS:
Electronic Book: 979-8-9862055-9-5
Hardcover: 979-8-9862055-7-1
Paperback: 979-8-9862055-8-8
Audiobook: 979-8-9862055-6-4

Cover design by Ashley Guillory
Author Photo Copyright Timothy Greenfield-Sanders

Printed in the United States of America
First Edition

Contents

Introduction	ix
My Shoes	xi

Part One: A Journey of Love   *1*
Somebody Kissed Me	3
My Girl	5

The Anne Poems   7
Desire	7
Evening	9
I Want to Love You as if You Have Never Been Loved	11
I Do	13
Dawn, the Seaside	15
Who is That?	17
Flower	19
Time to Go Home	21
Ghost Night	23
Our Home	25
Forever	27

The Liberty Poems   29
Liberty	29
The Light Eternal	31
My Pledge	33
Beautiful	35
Captured	37
My Ghost	39
How Can I Thank You?	41

Moving On   43
Tables Along the Sidewalk	43
A Tiny Memory	45
A Late Hour	47
In the Middle of Life	49

Part Two: The Journey of a Life — 51
The Lost Horse — 53

Going Home — 55
Home — 55
The House — 57
Memories — 59
Me and My Shadow — 61
In the Dreams — 63
She Walks These Hills in a Long Black Veil — 65
The Bicycle — 67
Dear Rat — 69
The Beasts of the Night — 71
A Funeral — 73
The Comets — 75
The Light — 77
An Old Man Walks Alone: A Song of the True Light — 79
A Strange Place Far Away — 81
One Tomorrow Soon — 83
A New Creation — 85

Words and Questions — 87
Lost Words — 87
The Word Rose — 89
Thought Questions — 91
The Hard Problem — 93
Digging for the Truth — 95

Falling and Flying — 97
Falling Angels — 97
The Only One Satan Doesn't Know is Himself — 99
And They Fell into the Fire — 101
Icarus Flies On — 103
Why Can't We Fly? — 105

Shadows of Life — 107
The Adventure of the Night when Everything is Gone — 107
Four O'clock in the Morning — 111
Glory — 113
Dearest Friends — 115

Poems about Poems — 117
The One that Got Away — 117
No Poem Today — 119
The Poem That Doesn't Work — 121

Four For Children — 123
A Fly — 123
Two Scorpions — 125
Mr. Potato — 127
Christmas — 129

Last Little Things — 131
I am a Poet of Small Things — 131
A Rainbow — 133
A Flea — 133
Creation — 133
Dancers — 133
Who? — 134
Two Friends — 134
Why? — 134

Introduction

The first section of this collection, "A Journey of Love," starts at the end: "Somebody Kissed Me" reflects the ongoing mystery and joy of a life lived side-by-side with the intimate and loving unknown that has been my lifelong and truest partner. Then it becomes a chronicle from first love through the discoveries that my dear Anne and I made together in "the Anne Poems" and how her parting felt, to a new experience explored in the "Liberty Poems," which are about one of the most sacred and difficult experiences ever to enter my life.

The second section, "A Journey of Life" involves explorations of the mysteries of beauty and tragedy that I see around me, and how it feels to be on my own journey of becoming a deeper, better man. These poems reveal a path that only they could light for me.

Then there are "Four for Children," emerging out of my love for those passing through that time of life.

The book concludes with a group of very small poems, into which the words came as if they had been there forever.

I've lived a hard and mysterious life, but I have also known love and joy beyond compare.

—Whitley Strieber

My Shoes

My poems are like me. They don't have stars.
They have shoes.
Not Florsheims, either. Just regular shoes like me.
I stepped in the morning grass and beads of dew
Blundered down the toes of my shoes.
The bus came.
The bus went.
I decided I'd call in and say
I have
A different life to do today.

PART ONE

A Journey of Love

Somebody Kissed Me

Deep last night somebody kissed me.
I'm an old man, and I live alone,
But somebody kissed me.
I'm not very pretty and was never
very pretty,
But they kissed me long.
I wondered at their breath,
Soft, cool and as sweet as death.
There was nobody here but me. There never is.
But somebody kissed me.
They kissed me long.
I reached up into the air, and found
Nobody there.
But still they kissed me, and kissed me long.
A night bird called, the leaves rustled, the curtains blew.
The night left me behind, and the kiss did, too.
I threw back the sheet and wondered what to do.
I don't belong to the sunlight and the day.
I'm an old man and belong to the night,
And that kiss. I belong to that kiss, too.

My Girl

Hand in hand we lay in the evening grass.
It was a simple thing, her hand in my hand as soft as a memory
Containing all time
And the shuddering of
Our desires.
I thought her eyes are brown, I thought
I'm—like that.
Will she does she know?
Ah, youth!
Fourteen, we were fourteen.
She said, star light star bright
I said, so high
Down at the end of the lawn the Vermillion River flowed
Louisiana, soft and full of yes, embracing us,
The Cajuns, the Evangeline Country, the swamp in its nakedness,
The children of the swamp with their alligator knowledge
Me pressing against her,
She whispering 'what's my secret?'
Me scared, slipping away, 'I don't know.'
The owls calling softly in the dark
The stars above them, the opossums whispering in the trees,
A radio across the street, soft voices of the south.
The south our home, our ghosts palely gathered,
We hand in hand, the Vermillion River flowing,
On it grumbling barges, silent men at their helms,

The stars above, the owls muttering,
Us, turning to each other.
Distantly a horn honks, slow laughter follows. Older kids.
We're hidden in the grass.
She whispers, 'kiss me.'

The Anne Poems

Desire

The women want us a certain way.
They want us to carry them
Down in the sheets.
They want us to give up everything to them
To expend ourselves for them
To lie then before them, towers become babes again.
They want us to be tall, to take their breath
With our power.
But then you see in their eyes
what they dare not say,
That they want us also little again,
To take delight in their glances
And be amazed by them,
For in our sons that they bear, they see us lying there,
Boys giggling and dreaming
Of the hidden flesh of the night,
That is their secret and their power,
And our delight.

Evening

The fan pulses overhead, outside a night bird murmurs.
She lays her hand upon me and laughs a little.
The leaves fluttering in the streetlight make our shadows dance.
She says, 'We are dreams.'
I make the only response I can: I am yours.
Her skin is as soft as a cloud, she is slow
In the soft of wife in the soft of lover.
I'm so glad I'm her man.

I Want to Love You as if You Have Never Been Loved

I want to love you as if you have never been loved,
As if you have never been
Except the love that I give you.
I want to live in the house of you.
I want to be a shadow there.
I want to be the footfalls on your journey.
Then when I sing the song of you,
My dangerous bird of night,
You will sail all the vault of the sky
Just to find me.

I Do

Hope waits
In my expectant heart.
It's raining, the roof drumming,
Thunder bouncing in the dark.
We sigh together
Riding the night.
Then at last you say, come to me,
Come here.
And I do.

Dawn, the Seaside

Her scent drifted toward me when the waves were long
And the night was nearly over,
When the moonlight made her body true,
And I lay alongside her
Like the moon on the last edge of the sea.
I so loved the way she tasted
When the first sun came,
Salt from yesterday's sea and dried wine on her lips,
And the way she felt beside me
While the sea boomed
And the moon swept low
And the holiness between us flowed,
River of heaven, wine of the night,
And a tiny secret stirred within,
Already bright with hope,
Unnamed but growing.
She says, 'I want an egg, I want water.'
I kiss the salt smooth skin of her arm while the gulls cry
And the sea foam shudders,
And she says, love, love, what might it mean?
We breakfast on sputtering eggs and pure water
And think no more of love.
But the ears within her hear our singing
And bring to it wonder, hidden deep.

Who is That?

Who is that just born?
Come forth, come forth you!
Come out from the shadows!
Your eyes are not quite focused yet,
But in their steady gaze,
There is all.

Flower

The sun again and breakfast again and we laugh again and
I say you are my flower and she says I'm dying.
She says it again, I'm dying, and I hear the hollow.
I say no flower and her eyes say—
And I say no flower flower no, oh flower flower
We hold and we hold and we hold and I say
Flower flower flower
And wouldn't the garden sing and the mountains ring
But no, we're just little in our little corner
Destined to be dragged apart by time and
The cascades of the body.
O flower flower may I come unto thee
O flower.
And her arms open and her smile opens
And we dare death together,
Wrapped in our arms,
In our bed
In the last of the night.

Time to Go Home

You lie whispering in this our room
Where the fan murmurs as it will when you are not here,
Where the sun streams as it will when you are not here,
Where the hummingbird brushes the sill
As it will when you are not here,
Where I sit where I will when your chair is empty.
You have said, time to go home.
Yes, yes, and may I come, too,
Do I have your leave?
I want to live in forever, just like you.

Ghost Night

I can find those evenings in my mind,
I can find those nights.
I can find that dress you cast away on the bedroom floor.
I can find moonlight on long skin and long thoughts
In moments that were too ordinary not to be eternal.
But now your laughter,
The most intimate thing I have ever known,
Slips away in the murmurs of the night.
The moon sets and our shadows join the dark.
Our bed is a ghost,
Your voice a remembered pleasure,
Your laughter lost in my losses.
Then I remember such a very sweet thing:
I, too, am gazing westward
At last.

Our Home

The light of the afternoon was just turning gold.
She pulled gently and
I walked out with her
And we walked in the flowers of the garden
And I said we will not see our garden again
And she said yes.
We walked along the shady summer street
And I said we will not see the shady trees again,
And she said yes.
Then I saw floating on the distance as if suspended
In magic, mountains greater than the Himalayas
And she said we are going there that is our true home.
And I said it looks so very far
Gently she drew me along
And looked back at me with her blue swimming eyes and said
Yes, our true home is very far.

Forever

The most beautiful thing in all my life
That I ever knew, was being with you.
It felt like it should be forever,
But time, that slippery angel,
Dropped you like a leaf onto the forest floor.
Then a breeze took you to live in the blue,
And I am here touching you,
Flying girl,
With you now in a new way,
And you with me, quiet and still,
Here to stay.

The Liberty Poems

Liberty

When first I saw her,
I thought she might mean liberty,
But I thought again when I took her hand,
For I knew that the opposite might be true for me.
She took me in songs I did not know were there,
And created in me a hidden well of wonder.
She led me to a closeness that I could not touch,
The most powerful kind,
And for the man I have become,
The best.

The Light Eternal

The light I saw in you was so pure that I thought
It must be light eternal.
Did it not race through the world forever,
Flowing from that window
Where you were singing earlier?

I thought, then, that your light eternal
Must go all the way to
The end of the world, and then
Live on as secret light beyond.

What a wonder to see such light
At play in your eyes.

Do you remember, when we walked in the forest,
You told me that your light eternal would be mine forever,
And would always make the flowers glow for me?

But I could not hold such fine light,
Not in my darker eyes.

It left me in an hour,
And went back to you.

My Pledge

I will always be with you when you want me
And always leave you when you want me gone.
I will wait in a corner in an alley under a tree
And sing the songs that you gave to me.
I will believe in your immortality
Even though I do not.
I will wait for a glance
Like a dog waiting for a bone.
I made myself yours and did not know it.
Now I can't get away,
For the collar has been locked,
And will remain so
For all my days.

Beautiful

I wrote a poem for you
And you didn't care.
Too wise, perhaps,
Or too joyous.
I died, then,
Anguished right down to my blood.
You listened to some music
And chatted with a friend,
And graciously let me go.

Captured

I have lost a sacred friend
And now it's night and I fear to lie down.
I thought her grand when her eyes flashed
And her voice blew through
Every room in the house.
I was happy when I was with her
But I am not that way now.
I have been captured by the joy she gave me
And must bear it within me
Forever.

My Ghost

These days pass easily for her,
And why not—
For her all days are new days,
Endless.
For me, every one
Is a new end.
I have said so many things to her
Since she left.
But nothing works.
She strolls on
Splendid with life.
I disappear
Into my own past,
And into hers.

How Can I Thank You?

How ever can I thank you,
Who gave me myself
By taking me from me?
You knitted me wings
That I could not see
Until you slipped away
So that I could fly free—
Which is why I call you
My liberty.

Moving On

Tables Along the Sidewalk

Tables along the sidewalk,
Two women sit, their faces huddled.
One cuts into a frittata, the other reflects silently.
A bus passes, shadows frozen within.
The wind soughs, the trees blow.
Little boys come along, running, shrieking.
Blood is remembrance,
Lives pass and it feels like an hour.
And then it's night and I'm back again.
Where the bus trundled, a coyote lopes,
A silent partner in the street.
The stars see nothing.
We only see the light
We cannot escape, nor the sounding night,
Nor any part of what we are,
Our eyes tossed about like waves,
The moon ripping at our skin,
Its shadows heartless in love.
And then it happens:
My deeper stars call to you.
You listen, you smile.
There is laughter then, a little.
And the night rolls on.

A Tiny Memory

Do you ever remember something very tiny
But so vivid that it makes you wonder what we are,
And from one another, how very far?
I was at a concert yesterday.
It was late and I was tired.
A few notes, no more than three,
Dropped me quite unexpectedly
Into eternity.
I had heard those notes played in just that way
Fifty years ago, if a day.
But what I remembered most was the harpist—
Not her face, I have forgotten that, or the melody
But the play of light on her fingers.
An hour later I saw her in the Blue Bar at the
Algonquin Hotel.
I was alone and so was she.
She sat and smoked a cigarette and drank a martini.
I did not speak to her nor she to me.
That's all there is, a tiny memory.

A Late Hour

Moonlight casts shadows that are questions.
Across the night, kisses flow.

On the distance, a dog mourns,
Nearer, a night bird whispers on her prowl.

A rat caught crossing a wire cries out,
The astonishment of death in his voice

In this cathedral of desire and terror
That is the living world.

Other voices, as soft as smoke,
Murmur love.

Babies squirm in the ocean of women,
In the realm of pleasure.

The tiny skeleton of a fallen wren
Lies in the sighing lawn.

Morning will bring the engine of the sun,
The rattle of the mower on the shuddering grass,
And the living will journey on.

In the Middle of Life

In the middle of life
I find the path curling.
The forest has gone
dark.
Memories of youth and warm skies,
our bed, the sounding ocean
the bells on the distance
ringing that all is well never
will this morning go.
You laughed do you remember
in the naked forever
the path quick
the sun always touching the dew.
But now your reflected eye
in the dark forest
is lost
and the path is curling.

PART TWO

The Journey of a Life

The Lost Horse

When the dancing is ended
And the lights are down,
And the long wind rises,

We enter a hidden path,
Remembering last things,
The note discarded, the photograph,
The chance.

How we danced!
We were fools in youth, of course,
All breathless and sure.

We made a high fire and had a good party.
But then, stepping out of the night,
Riderless,
Came the lost horse,
Ready for the journey.

Going Home

Home

Home. What does it mean?
Is it where we started or where we stop,
Or is it a more familiar place in between?
Home. It's where you can go
When you can't go anywhere else.
Home. It's those familiar curtains—
Remember mother's beige curtains?
And those voices—
Remember the children singing in the garden,
That's home.
And the birds singing all wild with life,
And your friends,
Dear to your heart,
Their voices close—
That's home.

The House

At night it sighs.
Blind though it is, it knows that
It carries precious sleepers in precious dreams.
The house once was trees, long strings of metal
That lived in the earth,
Dust and stone.
It carries those powers and also
The cat who sleeps in the sun
And the dog who wants water,
And the boy who comes back
Grown into a man, and says 'how small it all is.'
The little garden isn't much, either,
But it's the house's friend.
There are snapdragons in the spring,
And summer light brings roses.
Cooking, yes, there is cooking in the house, and eating.
Bodies slap together in the stirring night of the house.
Even the dogs dare to dream.
The house licks the faces of their secrets.
It knows also the secrets
The sun whispers in the morning window,
And the secrets of the people
Who wake up in sweaty sheets,
And of the ghosts who pass westward with
The rising of the day.

Memories

Memories are eternities made of dust.
They drift along the edges of our lives,
Calling as they must, for blessing and release.

A cat wandering the night may see them
Drifting in the half-light.

Cats don't understand them, though, only
That their drift is a curious thing.

Me and My Shadow

As I was having a walk in the night,
I watched my shadow slip out from under a streetlight.
My step seemed so very soft
That I wondered if I was there,
And then I knew—I was my shadow
And only that.
Where was my house?
I couldn't recall.
Was I watching the television there,
Reading a book?
How could I ever find myself
If I didn't know where I was?
Only my shadow knows,
And his whisper is too soft to hear.

In the Dreams

We who ride the waves of life
Think nothing of those who lie beneath,
The bones that danced and the crosses and the hairpins
That we buried with them, the rings, the other things,
That now lie tangled
In the dreams that were their lives.
They spoke so easily in this eternity of ours,
And drank coffee here with us and had ideas here,
And were supposed to be just like us,
Always here.

She Walks These Hills in a Long Black Veil

She walks these hills in a long black veil,
And visits my grave when the night winds wail.

Then I see her at Target buying another long black veil.
I guess the night winds got the last one.

Sure enough, the next night there she is again on the Elysian bus,
Headed for Holy Redeemer Cemetery.

I know I shouldn't, but I follow her.
And there she goes, off into the hills in her long black veil.

I think to myself, 'death, be not proud' as the night wind wails.

And here she comes again, standing over my grave.

Why did I buy the darned plot in the first place?
And how does she know it's mine, anyway?

Oh, death, death shall have no dominion--except, well, maybe
Life. Life is the dominion of death.

She strides off into the night wind with the clouds flying past the moon,
The long black veil snapping behind her.

I'm alone again.
I think I've been here a long time.
I love her, I know that, from some lighted room long ago.

I wish I could remember her name.

Thanks to John Donne, Dylan Thomas, Marijohn Wilkin and Danny Dill

The Bicycle

We are all waiting to die, she says.
Yes. Ok. I can see that.
That's what living is, she says.
Yes. Ok. I can see that.
Everything is waiting for that moment, she says.
There's a tension that never leaves anything.
Yes. Ok. I can see that.
Her father has just died. At the end he could not talk.
He grunted in code, furiously.
He was looking at that lampshade,
The one with the sailboats.
We couldn't understand. We don't know code.
Our son asked what happened to him.
She said, he was waiting and waiting to die and he did.
But why can't he say anything?
He is dead. He will no longer talk.
Our son thought about this. He said,
I don't want that to happen to me.
We are all waiting to die, she said.
Not me, he said. I have a bicycle and I know how to use it.
Later, he got a flat.
He cried and was furious. He beat the air with his little boy fists.
The bicycle lay in the sun.

Dear Rat

I have been watching a rat crossing a wire.
She doesn't know where she is,
Scurrying across all those conversations,
Between me and the moon.
I suppose an owl will take her soon.
What will she know then, flying?
What does she know now?
Certainly not that there are arguments
Racing beneath her feet,
Tales of sorrow and joy, sighs of love
And tired sighs, and counting, always that.
She knows none of these things, nor that the
Moonlight is perfect, and that it makes her pelt glow
In a way that pleases a monster she cannot see,
That is me.

The Beasts of the Night

Very late come the beasts of the night.
They are terrible to see, and you must not be found.
There are three of them
Over there near the ice cream store,
Where the shadows hang deep in that alley.
They speak together, words edged like knives.
The rain on their skin taps a dangerous code.
A silent hour, a squad car slides past.
A tense instant, but it doesn't slow.
Nobody likes that alley.
A crinkle of words from the dark, then whispered laughter.
It grows so late that one thinks almost of morning
With its drawn-up blinds and its coffee smells
And the little ones running and the birds
Busy in the day.
Over there near the ice cream store,
In that alley that nobody likes,
The sun turns the empty pavement to fire.
I join the day.

A Funeral

I saw a funeral passing by and thought, o my—
Then I thought—another world has died.
The hearse passed, a tired old thing.
Cars followed, a few.
They went down a street where flowers blew.
The sun was soft that day,
Children played, dogs ran, clouds flew.
It has been a long time since I saw that cortege,
Perhaps half my life or more.
Memory is so strange, what it retains,
The voices of the children, the flowers,
The tired old hearse, the surrendered life,
In one passing window, a shadow.
It must have been the wife.

The Comets

I saw my friends become elegant comets,
Spinning and quick.
And then my friends' friends
And their friends and down the sky road

Until they were a riot of comets, all bound away,
So bright that they were invisible,
Crowding the sky with tremendous harmonies.

The earth their mother had dropped them all,
The young, the old, the forgotten, the known—
All falling to the whispered song of the comets—
Destination unknown—
And then I saw by their light,
The flowers of night,
Pale blue and dancing
Beneath them all as they departed.

There were voices from that sweeping brilliance
Calling out little stories of the night,
of skin and shadows and dripping love,
That you would never think
Would be told by comets.

The Light

The light of pale voices,
Soft within us, glimmers in the petals of memory.

The light of pale voices,
Shines on the skin of a child
Woven out of air.

The light of pale voices
Is slow light, intimate in the voids of the night
And slow hands on the long bodies of long ago.

The light of pale voices
Is a spoken light that caresses and captures us all
Into the shuddering chamber of the inmost heart
That for want of a better word, we call life.

An Old Man Walks Alone: A Song of the True Light

An old man walks alone through a long life
Always forgetting
This world that is here to be forgotten.
He walks the pathway where the wind never stops,
The wind that calls the trees to fury
And shudders past the eves of the roadside tavern
Where it is his work to push a broom and sing a song,
and watch with his secret eye,
All the leaves of the past disappearing into the sky.
Far away, a long horn howls, a voice calls, 'Papa Dean, Papa Dean,'
But he's having no more of that.
He's on his way who has never had anything much
Or got to do anything much
But live among the stars in his head.
And oh so softly, so gently, infinity enfolds him
In its immense kindness,
And he feels for the first time, this son of a tragic girl
Long ago lost in the dust of the years,
That somebody is his friend,
Which is the whole immensity itself, all the stars.
So the stars in his head peek out and then come out
And the horn screams and the brakes wail their demon shriek
And then a call comes from above,
For the stars in his head to join the other stars.

In accusing red lights and running medics the raptured living
Look down upon a tatter and expanding blood.
'I couldn't do nothin.' He came outa nowhere.'
Nowhere? Not exactly that.
His stars know where.

A Strange Place Far Away

What is that strange blue place far below?
And why am I gazing at it as I do,
And what is this echoing thing I feel,
Is this love, this longing to be in
A quiet room with that ragged
Little shadow who huddles there
Calling a name again and again?
But I cannot hear the name.
And as for the ragged shadow
Kneeling beside the bed
In that struggle of tears,
What has she to do with me?

One Tomorrow Soon

There are women singing.
Their voices sound to me
Like treasures from the beyond.
I listen to the song
I listen to the clouds
I listen to the moon
I listen in their voices, to the dark.
I feel—
I cannot say it.
I feel as if I am already there.
The silence in their song is the most beautiful thing
I have ever known.
Somebody says: I think he's gone.
And I remember how I sailed
In a little blue boat when I was a boy.
I sailed until I lost the shore,
And then the sky,
And then the little pond I was on—
I lost that, too,
And sailed on.

A New Creation

There must have been a first day of light,
A first hour,
A first instant.

Was everything in it, then,
Every hair, every sigh,
Every facet of every eye?

Or did all of that come later,
As it exploded outward in wonder,
Making the ages and all the songs
Of all the worlds?

Is there one song that is the best song,
Perhaps lying forgotten on a paper
In some faraway edge
Where perfection lingers
Like an old friend who is always about to leave?

And what of the dogs and the dinosaurs
And the uncountable billions of strange dogs
And faraway dogs and the dinosaurs of other worlds?

Did the light know all of them at once,
Or did it guess creation?

Did it guess a woman tired in her kitchen,
Bursting with child and
Swabbing the floor with a dirty mop
And a head filled with roses?

Did it guess the struggle beneath the still mirror
Of the shimmering pond, the creatures scurrying for their lives
And does it know that it has left us in the fading ages
That swirl in the wake of its passing?

Does it know that each of us is here
And has always been here,
Even before it discovered itself.

We are each and all of us a trick of the light,
A gleam and gone.

Does the light know this? Does the light know
In the grandeur of its passing
That each of us is all we have?

Words and Questions

Lost Words

What has been lost in the languages that have been lost
Forever?
Did the leaves look different in different words?
Was the face of god made of other meanings?
And what of love, what are the lost words of love?
And where are the old intricacies of thought?
Are they hidden in the wind, waiting?
Or are they lost altogether, the words written
On secret skeletons that have no borders remaining
In the Earth,
Where all the words that have ever been
Lie waiting.

The Word Rose

Somewhere in some film or play or show,
I heard someone utter the word rose
More perfectly, I think
Than any other such utterance I know.
Rose, they said,
But who and where and when?
Those things I cannot recall.
Rose, the word rose.
Rose, they said, rose.
But where, in the shadows of my mind,
Did they go?

Thought Questions

I think I thought or thought I thought,
Or had thought.
There were questions about that, too,
Thought questions.
Like, is thinking about thinking thought
Or is it a thought, or was it?
Then I saw the sun on the floor.
I thought it was revealing dust
But it wasn't there.
The thought crossed my mind as
A cloud crossed the sky,
I thought in the wind.

The Hard Problem

The hard problem of consciousness
Is not explaining the stone,
But experiencing the stone
And all the attendant suspicions.
The detective returning with more questions
And soup on his necktie,
The hangman silent in the public house,
His own neck red
Where his collar has rubbed it—
The stone knows them both, but how?
The stone remembers the moon when it was a
New ghost in the sky, and rose to
The sighing expirations of the sea.
And dark things in the sea—the stone remembers them, too.
And ice and guttering tallow and silk
And penmanship and puttering motors,
And the hum of now.
The executioner lifts his glass like a machine.
Once he was a soft boy with pleading eyes.
Now they are as strange as the stone.
The stone is the hard problem.
All the rest, the detective suspects, is lies.

Digging for the Truth

Sometimes when you're digging for the truth
You find the truth.
But you're not expecting that
So you keep right on digging.
Soon you hear noises.
Then the whole hole collapses.
You land in a clatter of ceiling tiles and a spray of dust.
On the wall it says 23rd Street.
You're surrounded by practiced New Yorkers,
Skillfully pretending not to notice you
In your pajama bottoms, covered with dust.
But how did you get here?
You weren't in Manhattan.
And you were digging for the truth, not the IRT.
Then you see two transit cops coming toward you.
You've fallen into the Lexington Avenue Line
And that's the truth.
And those two cops are gonna arrest your ass.
You do the only thing you can.
You run.

Falling and Flying

Falling Angels

The angels falling

left in God behind them
grooves of memory.

As they passed us,
They also left behind all our stories
and all our songs,
the emerald of our voices
echoing in their history.

Passing into the downward that is outward
must be such an adventure, so enticing.

It must have made them what they have become—
God's dangerous children
on horses made of darkness
galloping forever across the thunder nights

Looking back and calling in their thunder voices,
can it be that bright—that far high bright—
is all of all goodness
in the house of God
our lost home?

The Only One Satan Doesn't Know is Himself

I fell, and I am.
I fell past my life that I knew,
My rain boots, my books, my luncheon on the table,
Sliced crisp carrots, hummus, pale cold wine.
I fell, and I am.
I fell past my son and my daughter,
Catching at their hands, calling to them,
'don't cry child,'
And they did not.
I fell, and I am.
I fell past the woman whose body I adore,
Past her warm skin and welcoming,
And I called out, 'goodbye, goodbye'
In the echo, fading.
I fell, and I am.
I fell past the tall waving grass and
I called out, 'goodbye grass, goodbye clouds above,
Goodbye, goodbye, goodbye—
I fell, and I am.
I fell past the newspaper I was holding,
The roses in the parlor,
The coffee and its tricky steam,
I cried out, 'o my God, save me.'
I fell, and I am.
I fell past the squalling babies
And the long stories.

And I heard the names,
I heard all of them, whispered by
The wind of my descent.
I fell, and I am.
I called out, 'goodbye, goodbye.'
My cries are swept away in the wind of my descent.
I see my son shooting hoops in the driveway.
I see my wife on the deck, her body rich in the sun.
My daughter reads in her room.
I hear the clock of life, but not for me.
I fell, and I am.
Where does it end,
Does it end,
This awful fall?

And They Fell into the Fire

The ants busy on the countertops
Fell into the fire.
The bees in the roaring glade
Fell into the fire.
The beetles clambering
Fell into the fire.
The opossums racing
The deer leaping
The blazing horses and cattle
The lovers in their snares
And the long lines of cars
All fell into the fire.
The doctors, speaking carefully,
Fell into the fire.
The moths raised their wings
In salute and
Fell into the fire.
The mothers rushing
Fell into the fire.
The children clinging
Fell into the fire.
The night birds with their dancing shadows
Fell into the fire.
The crawling things and the soaring things
Fell into the fire.
The fathers with their axes and their water

Fell into the fire.
The old and the very old and the thumping unborn
Fell into the fire.
The airplanes dropped from the flaring sky and
The grinding factories and
The dancing gardens
And the sweet houses
And the sounding coastlines
And the watchful trees
All fell into the fire.
And the fire went on and on and on.

Icarus Flies On

In Breughel's Icarus, as Auden says,
Everything turns away quite leisurely
But not from a disaster, as Auden thought,
For there is no disaster.
There is a forsaken cry from above, yes,
But that happens all the time now.
At first people were concerned by the boy's voice:
Help me, do something, get me down.
But like everything amazing,
It soon became uninteresting.
Whatever it represented, it was in the sky,
And what could matter up there?
It went on and on, help me, help me.
Perhaps white legs flailed above,
Or maybe it was a trick of the blowing clouds.
A delicate ship would sail past every morning
On its regular route.
Nobody looked up. Why should they?
The cries were simply part of the sky.
Every afternoon, the delicate ship would return.
The cries would echo and fade into the receding distance.
The next day it would happen again—
The delicate ship, the cries,
Nobody much caring except Icarus, trapped in the sky,
Flying on and on, crying out and flying on,
'Throw me a rope, help me,'
But nobody did or does.

The delicate ship has long since been replaced by
The Calais Hovercraft.
Everybody's inside drinking and toking and listening to rock and roll.
Icarus cries out, a boy in the sky,
Ignored, of no interest,
Lost in space and time.
Day and night, year by year, always,
Icarus cries out. Icarus flies on.

Why Can't We Fly?

I used to fly. My sister and I would fly.
Now I can't, and I want to fly.
We would fly over the roofs and higher.
She would steal cigarettes and we would
Light up among the clouds.
You had to be fast or the cigarettes
Would get wet.
You don't want to fly in the fields of heaven
With a wet cigarette.
That's no fun.
If God should see you, what would they think?
Or Jesus, that would be even worse--
You and your drooping cigarette.
Well, anyway we flew and we lit up and it was nice.

Shadows of Life

The Adventure of the Night when Everything is Gone

I couldn't sleep,
So I put on my slippers and went outside.

It was the quietest part of the night.

No birds chattered.
Nothing scrambled, snarled or screamed.
The sky was empty of owls, bats and planes.
But I did see some stars up there
Above the sacred oak.
Then I saw all the stars, even the stars you cannot see.
The sky was white with stars but the back yard was so dark
It was as if light hadn't been invented yet.

I wanted to see something,
Maybe a late skunk sniffing along,
Or that spider that lives under the porch railing.

But then I remembered that the oak had been cut down years ago.
It had bothered the neighbors with its swaying life and
Its sweet leaves, dropping in the autumn as if it was speaking
The true language of time.

There was no porch. There hadn't been one here in years.
There was no spider either, of course.

In fact, there was no lawn.
The house and its lot had been gone
Since before the past.

And who was I? I thought I'd had a name, but now that
Seemed to be gone, too.

Anyway, the stars can't look like that, not in this world.

I thought I'd better go inside and make some tea.

But then I remembered: the house is only a memory.
The tree is long gone,
The spider, the lawn.
And the stars can't look like this.

It is so quiet that I think that sound itself
Might be extinct.

I think it smells like snow tonight.
It did seem that way earlier.

I remember being a child here.
We used to sit under the tree that is gone
On the lawn that is gone
And make up adventures.

We would close our eyes and walk through the sleeping future
And look for things that were gone,
Feeling along the rows of memory, giggling and whispering.

We called this
The adventure of the night when everything is gone.

Four O'clock in the Morning

The street is mine, at this hour a river gone still.
A prowl car slides past, its radio muttering.
Old laughter floats from a dark house.
I know those people. They shop together,
Gray bobbing heads, rattling grocery basket.
I imagine them blinded by love at this hour,
Their bodies afloat in whispering sheets.

The street is mine, at this hour a river gone still.
There is no light in any window anywhere.
The moon is low. I know these shadows beneath
This old tree, they are friends of mine.
Destiny itself lives among them, sleeping now
With the sleeping rat and the insects stopped
In their wandering.

The street is mine, at this hour a river gone still.
Sensual death strolls behind me, lips cracked, eyes unseen.
A dog worries some trashcans, sniffing hopelessly.
There are clouds now, swift and pale,
Tumbling westward, slipping soft.
Memory embraces me, but so briefly that I cannot know
The shape of the past that it brings.

The street is mine, at this hour a river gone still.
On the thin horizon, a blush of pink.

A car pulls up to the house where the young models live,
Its motor breathing, its lights stirring the waters of the night.
A girl comes clicking toward it, her shoulders hunched
Under a long black coat.

The car slides away, the roofs of houses define themselves
Against the east of dawn. A wren awakens and chitters.
A young man comes towering past, his sneakers slapping the sidewalk.
'Morning, he says.

Yes, I think to myself, but that's not all it is.

Glory

In my grocery store,
The cereal boxes stand sentinel
before the dark at the back of the shelves.
In the produce department, the drip lines make the
Tomatoes glimmer and the kale shiver and the skin
Of the peppers
Reflect our passing eyes.
The fish counter smells of the
Death of the sea.
The man behind it all in white
I will later see out back smoking and staring.
I wonder if he, too, feels the naked heave of our store,
Filled with staring fish, nameless, meaningless,
To be filleted and forgotten?
At the meat counter, I hear the uneasy bleating of mystified lambs,
And the shrieks of pigs
and cattle booming from their boxcars
as they rattle across the prairie night.
I see the red flat wonder of their meat, and I know
That down below where I cannot go, the holy cellar rats
Lick the dripping blood, their tongues as quick as mayflies.
Long wheat fields, drenched in the past, slip into the
Bakery department, into the aisle lined
With cakes and cookies and cupcakes swirled with
White icing and pink icing and chocolate icing.
A child begs from the back of his mother's cart
For just a taste.

In his movements and in his eyes
I see all the children, the fat and the lean,
The fed and the tattered and the ones who smile
And the ones who don't.
In our store there is a lottery machine, too, deep in the dark.
There are dreams at its feet,
Little puddles shimmering like old grease.
Past the end of our parking lot,
Past the pharmacy and the yogurt store that are there,
the bluff ends our town at the tidal edge of America.
Beyond it spreads the ocean, and in its deep
I hope that there are things of which we know nothing,
which will never land on our dark shore,
and whose pale flesh will never be handled by us.
The ocean flows and evening glows and comes the night,
And the aisles of our store grow dim.
Then morning follows,
And the lumbering white-sheathed ghosts
Return, as do I.
I forgot toilet paper and popcorn and mint jelly.
A shaft of sunlight follows me in, but as quickly withdraws.
The registers clatter, I descend.
The dark aisles enclose me.
Then comes the distant thud of a switch and
Neon flaps on, as bright as an exploding bomb.
Shopping music makes us rush and
My heart says glory. Oh, glory.
There's the mint jelly!
Such things—obscure things like that—are so often
Hard to find.

Dearest Friends

I want a secret place in a forest
That is by the sea
Where I can be absolutely alone
And listen to the rioting of the water
And the prayers of the leaves in the trees
And the gossipy birds
And the strange things that boom in the sea.

Then I want to invite the dearest friend in the world
Whomever that may be.
Then I want to invite their dearest friend
And their dearest friend
And their dearest friend
And all the dearest friends of the dearest friends
In the world
Until all the dearest friends
Have come to my place near where
The waves riot
And the leaves pray
And the birds gossip
And strange things boom in the sea.

And we'll talk of happiness
And it will grow dark
And the sea will become still
And birds will fall silent

And the leaves will stop,
And the booming will go deep,
And we'll be all of us together,
In our secret place that is in the forest
That is by the sea, and ours alone.

Poems about Poems

The One that Got Away

I've got a poem running around in me that I can't catch.
It's been chasing my grocery list all day.
Kale. Hoover rug cleaner. Peanuts.
That's not the poem, though. That's where it hides.
A poem is something blue and deep
That you can't quite figure out.
Comet cleanser.
Old eyes that say we're perfect
But don't know it.
Rice-a-Roni, bottle of pickles,
Girl singing in the night.
Perfection everywhere, in a discarded coke bottle,
In the voices outside the yogurt place,
The wind rising, my poem escaping the list,
And rising also, into the swaying stars.

No Poem Today

I thought I would write a poem today,
But nothing came to mind save the way the light
Spreads in the morning
And the dew rises from the grass.
Not much poetry in that, or running deer,
Or fog soldiers marching down the dawn-lit river.
Then I thought of Rice Krispies smiling in a bowl,
And my little son listening in wonder to their famous crackle.
He is enveloped in the sweetness and noise of his childhood.
He asked me, why are flowers flowers
And not something else?
That was when I thought a poem would come to me,
But all that came was a little boy and a bowl of cereal,
And the sunlight streaming in the kitchen window.
He asked me, if we can't tell if a secret is secret,
How do we know that it is?
I said, if a secret is secret, then we can't know even that it's there.
He said, I have a secret that's there.
What is it, then, I asked him.
He said, it's a secret, so I don't know. But it's there.

The Poem That Doesn't Work

Here I am back again fooling with the poem that doesn't work.
A poem needs a certain structure. It needs the just right words.
And that's why this is the poem that doesn't work.
Mikey from across the street informs me that there is a bear
In our garden.
I say, "we have a big garden."
He says, "that isn't important."
This poem is that kind of bear.
Get those pants off the line my wife says, it's gonna storm.
Going to, actually. This is a poem. You say going to, not gonna.
The sun crosses the zenith. There are stars above the blue.
Blue. It's a word that sounds like what it is. Azure.
The twins come in and announce that there is an ouroboros in the garden.
Sort of like the bear, I guess. And the poem that doesn't work, of course.
There comes a time in life when you know what isn't.
Then you're not a child anymore.
My twins who are almost there both want to be hugged at the same time.
They explain that the ouroboros says I have to,
Which is also why the poem doesn't work.
The path of this poem is an ouroboros
Made of twins,
And they are in my arms.

Four For Children

A Fly

On my slice of pie, a pregnant fly.
She is busy with the sugar glaze
 And a bit of cherry.
Always hungry, I'm sure, carrying all those babies.
If I swat her,
Then her little ones also must die.
Her many lensed eyes reflect me,
Watching carefully.
Her wings flutter, busy, nervous.
She knows she's despised.
But not by me.
I have fallen in love with her
And her pulsing belly
And the little bit of hope that somehow in all
The great vault of the world,
The clouds, the speeding days, the stars,
That little bit of hope that is what she carries
Of the vast of life.

Two Scorpions

They saw looming death,
A terrible shadow,
That was me.

They ran for the drain
And cowered there in
Its illusion of safety.

The light I had turned on
Made them shine,
Their tan segmented stingers
Raised in hopeless threat.

They were face to face,
As if embracing
With their ugly claws.

Were they husband and wife,
Sister and brother, or simply
Two friends who'd been
Out for a stroll?

Now death had come to them
And they awaited my pleasure.
What did their simple eyes see,
What hopes did they harbor,
What losses dread?

These ugly, dreadful things
badly wanted to live,
It was so clear.
But I knew I must kill them.
What of the children and
Their little fat feet?

They waited.
I considered.
For them the light would darken,
The stingers would whip,
Their crushed lives would be tossed
Indifferently into the toilet.

As I thought of these things,
I watched them, as still as two
Ugly little stones.
They watched me, too, I am sure.
What meaning did I have for them,
Only the crushing of the shell, the tearing of
Precious muscles, the exploding of the heart.

I captured them in a washcloth
And took them outside
And released them into the grass.

Mr. Potato

"When to the sessions of sweet, silent thought,
I summon up remembrance of things past,"
What comes first to mind is usually Mr. Potato.
When he arrived in our neighborhood, he was the only dog
Who was long and low.
When he departed from this life fourteen years later,
All the younger dogs in the neighborhood
Were long and low.
On the way home from the dog farm,
He tore his way out of his box and attacked my left arm.
Once we got home he started barking to protect somebody,
Maybe even us, from harm.
He ran everywhere with us, and when he was too slow
On his little legs short and low,
To keep up with us he would roll.
What you did with a ball was Mr. Potato's call.
If you had candy, he thought that was dandy.
If you cried, he danced at your feet and gave it his all.
One day the bus driver came up the yard.
He was in tears, he had Mr. Potato in his arms.
'Boys,' he said, 'I killed Mr. Potato, I'm so sorry.'
Clearly, Mr. Potato had come to fatal harm.
We dumped him in a bag, leaped on our bikes
And rushed him to the emergency room.
The nurse said, 'take him to the vet,'
But a kindly doctor gave him a shot that reversed his doom.
He came back to life just like that.

From then on he was a little baggy but
He still took all the balls and ate all the candy,
And danced for you when you were feeling badly.
Years passed and here came the bus driver again,
Mr. Potato once dead again in his arms.
He was crying so hard he could hardly see.
 By this time we had cars and Mr. Potato's snout was gray.
We figured what the hell and took him to the vet anyway.
He came back to life on the examining table.
It scared the vet but he was happy, too.
He said I think your old dog is held together by glue.
Mr. Potato would wait on the porch for our return.
I got married and Jack did, too.
Come July the Fourth, the family gathered,
The wives, the kids, the mothers, the fathers.
As always Mr. Potato worked toward the hot dogs, slinking low.
We let him do it,
He worked so hard and by this time moved so slow.
Then plop, he went down.
His legs folded, his head hit the ground.
We rushed him to the vet but this time is was no go.
Dr. Carruthers said, 'I think Mr. Potato's been dead
For at least ten years. He just didn't know.
Inside, there was really nothing left but goo.'
I wasn't surprised, he had boys to raise and bitches to seed.
There was simply too much to do.
Sometimes when I'm home I think I hear him barking in the back yard,
And mom is convinced that he somehow still pees on the rug,
Just to remind her who ran this show—
Dad, sure, and her,
But also that long dog, long ago.

Christmas

Three days and one after the sun begins to return,
Fires are lit on the gathered snow, dancing starts
Because they know
The world will continue somehow, the sun's excursion is done.
They dream of the waving wheat, while stomping in the blowing snow.
The Romans feasted on last summer's food,
Why not? More would come and soon.
But then there's Bethlehem, a child is shining born,
And shepherds are perplexed by mysterious transits in the night.
Tiny, warmed by the breath of cattle, mother not yet wed,
A family desperate with mystery,
The shepherds coming, eyes turned inward to the wonder they have seen,
The father afraid, what will happen to my son?
Is he my son?
And my wife—what does her story mean?
They're in a cave behind an inn, nobody cares, he's a bit of flesh
Wrapped in a thin old cloak, hardly there at all.
Just another babe, but the only one born here tonight,
So what were those lights?
He lives a hard life and dies a miserable death.
He's here now, only waiting to be noticed again
As he was then, just briefly, by a few perplexed shepherds.
Christmas lights, 'twas the night before, Jolly St. Nick, presents
Under the tree, children shuddering with glee,
Cookies and candy and cinnamon spiked brandy,
Half a billion trees, ornamented and dying,

Children afraid that their lists will be ignored for their lying.
Then the morning and he came, Santa despite the snow and rain.
X-Boxes, iPads, books galore, roses, toy trains,
Watches and neckties, spun sugar and video games,
The church all swarming with squirming kids, the priest pronouncing,
Them wishing he was done,
All the joy of the day, the quiet of the afternoon, the wonder we
Have made, the miracles accomplished,
And back there in the past, the shadow of another life, now long over,
Whose gifts linger yet, in our compassion, our love, our humble souls.
He gave us those.

Last Little Things

I am a Poet of Small Things

I am a poet of small things,
A flower sleeping in the sun,
A child's hungry grin,
Dew pearling a branch in the morning,
Bitterns booming in the marsh,
Hands held and hands refused,
Lost pathways rich with the scent of life.
I am a poet of small things,
Things too small to remember
Drifting like dust in morning light.

A Rainbow

Splashing through puddles
The storm left behind
A rainbow in my shoes.

A Flea

A flea on my wrist
Too small even for a tiny poem
But still there.

Creation

Maybe God considers
Creation a haiku.
Stars, lives, then gone.

Dancers

Kids were dancing in the alley.
I asked them why.
They said, 'we're dancing dancing.'

Who?

The moon hides tonight
The trees sigh
Who died?

Two Friends

I contemplate Kali Ma
She contemplates me back
Danger ahead.

Why?

There always comes a moment
When we must say goodbye.
So goodbye.
But why?

www.ingramcontent.com/pod-product-compliance
Lightning Source LLC
Chambersburg PA
CBHW051621010526
44119CB00033B/436/J